Ex€
yo

Enjoy Your Prayer Life

Michael Reeves

Series Editor: Michael Reeves

Copyright © 2014 by Michael Reeves and 10Publishing

First published in Great Britain in 2014

The right of Michael Reeves to be identified as the Author of this Work
has been asserted by him in accordance with the Copyright, Designs
and Patents Act 1988.

British Library Cataloguing in Publication Data
A record for this book is available from the British Library

ISBN: 978-1-909611-64-1

Designed and typeset by Pete Barnsley (CreativeHoot.com)

Printed in Denmark by Nørhaven

10Publishing, a division of 10ofthose.com
Unit C, Tomlinson Road, Leyland, PR25 2DY, England

Email: info@10ofthose.com
Website: www.10ofthose.com

3 5 7 10 8 6 4 2

Contents

Let Michael Reeves nourish and encourage your prayer life! I warmly commend this book to you.

Paul E. Miller,
Author of *A Praying Life*

The Problem With Prayer

This is not a new revelation but sadly most of us are not good at prayer. That's the state of Christianity in the West right now, and it is concerning. Moreover, it seems even church leaders are not communing with God much. How healthy can their churches or fellowship groups be if this is the case? The fear is that parallels will slowly develop with the church in Corinth. There, through Paul's letters, you see the leaders of the church commending themselves, peddling God's word insincerely, and being fleshly not spiritual, proud, hypocritical and competitive. Their prayer-life was shameful, for clearly love for Christ and dependence on him had been eclipsed by self-love and self-dependence.

Prayerlessness always goes hand in hand with a lack of Christian integrity. This is even more so for Christian leaders – to put it bluntly, if they are not enjoying communion with God, then they are selling a product they don't really believe in. All that's compounded by the fact that – I know how easily – the importance and urgency of what they do can, ironically, collapse into self-sufficient busyness, causing them to be a bunch of Marthas (see Lk. 10:38–42). So as they groom themselves to be successes at Christian life and mission, there's a vacuum when it comes to their actual communion with God. Now I stress strongly that I'm speaking as one failure to another. Nevertheless, in the light of this real concern about our prayerlessness, I hope this book will be a refreshment and a tonic – maybe even a kick-start! – for our prayer lives.

> *'Prayerlessness always goes hand in hand with a lack of Christian integrity.'*

What is Prayer?

We need to think first about what exactly prayer is. This may sound silly, but I think confusion over it is a real cause of much of our difficulty. The reality is that it's very easy to think and speak about prayer as if it's some abstract exercise – one of those 'things Christians "do"'. And so we think: how can I get better at this thing called prayer? Now if you do think of prayer like that, as a thing on its own, the solution to a better prayer life is always going to be practical tips and techniques. So, for example, you sort out a prayer diary, get a prayer list app for your phone, use Operation World, try praying out loud, and have your quiet time first thing in the morning. I specifically mention those things because I think advice like that is genuinely helpful ... in its place. However, that's not the heart of prayer.

Furthermore, if those techniques are what hold together 'prayer' for you, then it's going to be a burdensome duty – or perhaps something that even veers towards magic, whereby you think you can get what you want by saying the right 'spell'. (And if you don't get the answer you want, you begin to question whether this magic 'formula' actually works.) The Lord says of Israel, 'These people come near to me with their mouth and honour me with their lips, but their hearts are far from me' (Is. 29:13). Thus prayer is not an abstract 'thing to do', for clearly you can 'do' prayer and get it all wrong. There is something vital underneath all the pragmatics. So what is prayer? It's never been put better than by John Calvin, who in his excellent little chapter on prayer in the Institutes calls prayer 'the chief exercise of faith'. In other words, prayer is the primary way true faith expresses itself. This also means that prayerlessness is practical atheism, demonstrating a lack of belief in God.

Help!

While I'm saying that it is great to define prayer as 'the chief exercise of faith', my first reaction to this is to think: O my Lord, how faithless am I!

In one sense your prayer life is disgustingly revealing: it does reveal who you really are. For all your talk and theory of faith – you can affirm the truth of prayer and know *that* God is good – your prayer life reveals how much you *really* want communion with God and how much you *really* depend on him. I stress it absolutely does not tell you about your security as an unrejectable child of God, but it does tell you, very accurately, how much of a baby you are spiritually, how much of a hypocrite you are, and how much you actually love the Lord. Thus if your tendency is to think you're rather wonderful, just remember your prayer life.

Yet don't be dismayed! Yes, it means you need to start at the beginning in learning how to pray. But if prayer is 'the chief exercise of faith', then of course you're naturally rubbish at prayer, because you're naturally lacking in faith. If prayer is 'the chief exercise of faith', then of course everything – the world, the flesh and the devil – conspires against prayer. This means that you're not the odd one out in your struggles with prayer, and it's not your secret shame – which can be the crippling fear. You're just a sinner, naturally inclined away from faith and prayer. We're all sinners. And you know who the friend of sinners is! Jesus.

'... you're naturally lacking in faith ...'

We're All Sinners

I find, particularly when I'm thinking of prayer as an abstract exercise, it's so easy to forget that basic dynamic of the gospel and then wonder what it is I'm missing in prayer. This is where I think we can be unmanned by those fearsome stories of 'the great prayers'. Have you heard, for example, that apocryphal story of Martin Luther? Apparently he was asked one evening what he'd be doing the next day and he replied, 'Work, work from early till late. In fact I have so much to do that I shall spend the first three hours in prayer.' Tales like this turn our bones to jelly because we know we're not like that.

So to prove we are *all* sinners, and therefore naturally awful at prayer, here's a real quote from Luther that will comfort you. At perhaps the busiest time of his busy life he wrote to his friend Philipp Melanchthon:

> *You extol me so much … Your high opinion of me shames and tortures me, since – unfortunately – I sit here like a fool and hardened in leisure, pray little, do not sigh for the church of God … In short I should be ardent in spirit, but I am ardent in the flesh, in lust, laziness, leisure, and sleepiness … Already eight days have passed in which I have written nothing, in which I have not prayed or studied; this is partly because of temptations of the flesh, partly because I am tortured by other burdens.[1]*

Even Luther, a man who valued prayer very highly, was a real person, a real sinner. We're all sinners.

---

1. *Luther's Works, vol. 48*, p. 256.

Prayer Springs From God's Word

Let's leave Luther and come back to Calvin and his definition: prayer as the chief exercise of faith. Now if that's true, what is going to help us sinners pray? Remember, prayer is about faith. So where does faith come from? It comes from hearing the word of God. As Paul wrote, 'Consequently, faith comes from hearing the message, and the message is heard through the word about Christ' (Rom. 10:17). Faith – and so prayer – is birthed by the gospel. That's why scripture and prayer are so often put together.

We see this connection illustrated by Daniel. As he was reading the book of Jeremiah, his insight from it prompted him to pray. 'In the first year of Darius ... I, Daniel, understood from the Scriptures, according to the word of the Lord given to Jeremiah the prophet, that the desolation of Jerusalem would last seventy years. So I turned to the Lord God and pleaded with him in prayer and petition, in fasting, and in sackcloth and ashes' (Dan. 9:1–3).

It is the word of God, the gracious message of Christ, that awakens faith and so prayer – and so that must be the basic shape of our everyday communion with God. We need to set Christ before ourselves. That is, we hear the word of Christ in Scripture, in song, through each other and by reminding ourselves as we praise him. We should long that our eyes might be opened to see the beauty of the Lord and that we might be drawn afresh to want him – and then prayer is simply the articulation of our heart's response.

To summarise what we have discovered so far, prayer is the chief exercise of faith. Naturally we're rubbish at prayer because we're sinners. Yet the solution – what will give us the true life of real communion with God – is the gospel of Christ that awakens faith.

Praying Like Jesus

Here's where we come to the magic doorway. When you come to Jesus, prayer changes. Familiarity blinds us to the wonder of this, but there's something extraordinary about Jesus. Jesus is the Lord; he is Immanuel, God with us. But *our Lord and God prays*. In fact he's always praying. When full of joy, he'd pray; when agonising, he'd pray; when making major decisions like appointing apostles, he'd spend a good bit of time in prayer. His prayer inspired his disciples to ask, 'Lord, teach us to pray' (Lk. 11:1).

Yet Jesus' prayers are not just significant because he's praying on earth as the model human. No, he's also showing who, eternally, he is. John tells us, 'Very truly I tell you, the Son can do nothing by himself' (Jn. 5:19). The Son always depends on his Father; that is who he eternally is. For him, everything flows from his communion with his Father. And so for eternity he has enjoyed communion with him and he has prayed to him.

The Son, then, is the first pray-er. And the salvation he brings is a sharing of his own communion with his Father. *Prayer is learning to enjoy what Jesus has always enjoyed.*

Praying to God as Our Father

With that, we come back to Luke 11: 'One day Jesus was praying in a certain place. When he finished, one of his disciples said to him, "Lord, teach us to pray, just as John taught his disciples." He said to them, "When you pray, say: *Father* …"' (Lk. 11:1, my emphasis). The first thing Jesus would have pray-ers know is the name Father. That's the first and basic lesson in prayer. The relationship he has always had with his Father he now shares with us – and it transforms prayer. Our instinct is to think of the Almighty in holy transcendence – God without Christ. But Christ has brought this holy God to be our open-armed Father. Thus Jesus invites us – in fact, commands us! – to pray 'our Father'.

Jesus is telling us to remember always who God is – our Father. Moreover, to our Father, prayer is as incense; it is a pleasing smell to him. In other words, he delights to hear and help us.

If you read on in Luke, you will notice that straight after teaching his disciples the Lord's Prayer, Jesus continues by saying to them, 'Suppose you have a *friend*, and you go to him at midnight and say, *"Friend ..."*' (Lk. 11:5, my emphasis). Praying is enjoying – and pleading for – the friendship and friendly assistance of God. You then see in Luke's account that the friend doesn't immediately answer and give the bread, for we are to understand that our heavenly Father and Friend wants us to persevere in our prayers. Of course, God could give to us and bless us without our asking – and how he regularly does that in his grace! But the God of fellowship wants fellowship with us. He wants us to argue his promises and his character with him, for then who he is becomes an ever more conscious reality for us. We grow as we persist – developing in our appreciation that he is our Friend, that he is the source of all blessing, and that we and the world need him to be put right. You therefore see repeatedly in the

Old Testament that when Israel no longer called out to him, he wouldn't help them. For he wants us to know that blessing comes only from him. Blessing is not natural, and ultimately it can be found nowhere else.

Just look how Jesus keeps pressing the kind fatherliness of God: 'Which of you fathers, if your son asks for a fish, will give him a snake instead?' (Lk. 11:11). Even we wicked fathers don't give our children vials of anthrax when they come to us, even we are kind – how much can we expect of the Father of lights, in whom there is no darkness at all! There's something similar written in Isaiah. The Lord says, 'Can a mother forget the baby at her breast and have no compassion on the child she has borne? Though she may forget, I will not forget you! See, I have engraved you on the palms of my hands' (Is. 49:15–16).

Jesus is stressing that the willing and attentive kindness of our God is essential to know for prayer. We instinctively think of God without Christ – merely as Lord and Judge. And then we feel he'll not want to hear from us sinners – and we won't want in our guilt to be in his presence.

But when we remember his friendliness, his open-armed fatherliness – that he has adopted us – it makes us want to go to him.

Jim Packer once wrote, 'If you want to judge how well a person understands Christianity, find out how much he makes of the thought of being God's child, and having God as his Father. If this is not the thought that prompts and controls his worship and prayers and his whole outlook on life, it means he does not understand Christianity very well at all.'[2] Packer's right, for to address God as Father *and mean it* is to understand the gospel well. It means you understand that the Son, who has been eternally 'in the bosom of the Father' (Jn. 1:18, as translated from the original Greek), has come to bring us that we might be with him there, and that we who have rejected him might be brought back – and brought back not merely as creatures but as children, to enjoy the abounding love the Son has always known. To know you are a beloved child of God protects you from thinking of prayer as a ladder to God

2. Packer, J.I., *Knowing God* (London: Hodder & Stoughton, 1973), p. 224.

or an exercise by which you work your way into his favour. Prayer doesn't make you more accepted. Instead, prayer is growing in the appreciation of what you *have been given*. It may be that your heart is cold, your love is weak and your prayers are shabby, but what matters is that, united to Christ and in him, you are a cherished son – and your Father delights to hear you. Of course, with any other God we'd have to come in the strength of our own fervour; with this God we come in his.

John Calvin said that we pray, as it were, through Jesus' mouth. The Father has always longed to hear the prayers of his dear Son – and we pray in his name. The Son gives us his name to pray in so that we pray *as him*. That relationship between the Father and the Son is what we have been brought in to enjoy – and in prayer that's what we do. So, once again, prayer is exercising faith – believing God's almost incredible promise that we *can* come to him, even though our coldness and

> '... *It may be that your heart is cold, your love is weak ...*'

17

guilt screams otherwise. We must believe the Most High is our loving Father. And that is prayer: relating to the Father as our Father.

Of course, we have a personal relationship with the Son and the Spirit as well, and so we can pray to them. But *normal* Christian prayer is something richer and juicier: we join in with the fellowship of God as the Father, Son and Spirit are already enjoying it. We're brought into that communion. Thus the Son – who is already interceding for us with his Father – brings us to be with him before his Father. While under Old Testament law the high priest would go into the presence of the Lord in the Holy of Holies *on behalf of* the rest of Israel, the Son *takes us* before his Father – and there the Spirit helps us.(We will look more at the role of the Spirit in a moment.)

8

Praying at All Times

If prayer is communion with God, then it can take many forms. We have different sorts of conversations with our friends and families – from texts and emails to rambling chats late into the evening. Similarly, we don't need to try to 'fit' God *into* each day, that is to see our prayer life as something different from the rest of life. In fact the danger arises precisely when you do think your prayer life is something separate. No, for the Son everything flows from his communion with his Father, and so it should become for us. When you know that each day is already all God's and that we have fellowship with him all the time, then prayer suffuses the whole day more naturally. Then you find yourself intuitively praying through the day more, and without feeling the need to be hyper-spiritual and concentrated the whole time. For me, very often it's unclear whether I am praying at a particular moment or working; it is both at the same time. Even in times when I've settled down just to pray, almost every day I find that the Lord answers at least one prayer for wisdom and guidance immediately and I have to note it down or act on it before I can carry on praying. We have communion with God at all times. However, having said that, relationships only grow when you give each other quality time. And here's one way I hope what we've seen will improve your quiet times. When you default to thinking of prayer as an abstract activity, a 'thing to do', the tendency is to focus *on the prayer* as an activity – which makes it boring. Instead, focus *on the one to whom you're praying*. Reminding yourself *who you are coming before* is a great help against distraction, and changes the prayer. That's just

> '... **We have communion with God at all times ...'**

what happens in the Psalms – they constantly interrupt their own petitions to speak of the Lord's faithfulness and kindness. So should we, and persistently focusing again on him then elicits more earnest and hearty prayer.

9

Depending on God

Prayer is enjoying that the Father really is our Father. But what exactly does it mean that God is a Father? First, it means he is eternally begetting his Son. Always he is giving life to and lavishing his love on his Son. So, as Father, he is the source of all life, love and blessing. And what does it mean to be the Son? Eternally, the Son is characterised by receiving from the Father. Now if that's the relationship we've been brought into, then praising the Father as Jesus did, asking the Father for things as Jesus did and depending on the Father as Jesus did are going to be staple parts of our communion with him. By thanking him and praising him, we acknowledge his kindness and greatness, that he is good and that all good truly comes from him. By asking him for things, we exercise our belief that he really is the fountain of all good and that without him we can do nothing that is actually good.

If God was a single, independent person, independence would be the godly thing. That would be how to be like him. But as the Son always depends on the Father, that is the nature of Christian godliness. Being a Christian is first and foremost all about receiving, asking and depending. It's when you don't feel needy (and so when you don't pray much) that you lose your grip on reality and think or act in an unchristian manner. In fact, as you grow as a Christian, you should feel not more self-sufficient but ever more needy. If you don't, I'm not sure you're growing spiritually. If you really feel your need to depend on God, though, prayer will simply flow from this.

'as you grow as a Christian, you should feel not more self-suffcient but ever more needy'

Prayer, then, is enjoying the care of a powerful Father, instead of being left to a frightening loneliness where everything is all down to you. Prayer is the antithesis of self-dependence. It is our 'no' to independence and our 'no' to personal ambition. It is the exercise of faith – that you need God and are a needy receiver. With this in mind, instead of chasing the idol of our

'Prayer is the antithesis of self-dependence'

own productivity, let's be dependent children – and let the busyness that could keep us from prayer *drive* us to prayer. Only then – like the Son – can we actually be fruitful.

The Spirit Helps Us

The Son has brought us to be with him – in him – before his Father. That's what we enjoy in prayer. But what about the role of the Spirit? Well, the Son does all that he does in the power of the Spirit. In creation, the word of God goes out on the Spirit or breath of God. So we read in Genesis that the Spirit hovers (Gen. 1:2), and in his power God's word goes out, for example with the command 'Let there be light!'(Gen. 1:3). Jesus starts his ministry at his baptism by being sent out into the wilderness by the Spirit. He expels demons by the power of the Spirit. The Spirit is also the one who stirs up the Son to commune with the Father. For example, Luke records that 'Jesus, full of joy through the Holy Spirit, said,

'I praise you, Father' (Lk. 10:21). That is the Spirit's work in the Son, and that is his work in the children of God. The same principle is explained in Romans. 'For those who are led by the Spirit of God are the children of God. The Spirit you received does not make you slaves, so that you live in fear again; rather, the Spirit you received brought about your adoption to sonship. And *by him we cry, "Abba! Father."* The Spirit himself testifies with our spirit that we are God's children' (Rom. 8:14–16, my emphasis). The Spirit drives the Scripture-taught truth of our adoption by God into our hearts so we know that we are his children, and thus we cry, 'Abba!' The Spirit is the wind in the sails of our prayer as he catches us up into the Son's love for the Father. Making us know we too are loved, he causes us to love as the Son loves. Prayer, then, is not actually a one-way conversation, us to God. No, in prayer God speaks through us to God.

'The Spirit is the wind in the sails of our prayer'

We're brought into the divine fellowship. The

Spirit of the Son cries to the Father through us.

Paul then goes on: 'In the same way, the Spirit helps us in our weakness. We do not know what we ought to pray for, but the Spirit himself intercedes for us through wordless groans' (Rom. 8:26). That's an enormously helpful verse if you're interested in genuine communion with God. The Spirit knows that we're weak, that we struggle to pray and that we often don't know what to pray – and his desire is to help us. This means that we don't need to pretend to be giants in prayer or make resolutions that are out of our league. Since the Spirit knows our weakness, we can be real with our Father, accepting how babyish we are in our faith, and simply stammer out what's on our hearts. In fact, that's just the way to grow in our relationship with God. True intimacy is an acquired thing, something that develops – but it only develops with honesty. So if your prayer life is a bit ropey, I suggest starting again by stammering like a child to a Father. Cry for help. Don't try to be impressive.

11

The Spirit Makes us Christ-like as we Pray

Another thing the Spirit does is to transform us to be like Christ. He helps us to be dependent and prayerful, and by bringing us into the Father–Son relationship he brings us to share God's life *and purpose*. Our desires start echoing God's, his passions become ours, and so we begin to share his love and compassion for his people and his world. Consequently, we become intercessors and priests, like our great high priest Jesus who is constantly interceding. The Spirit works to make us like Christ in that respect. There's an interesting little moment in Matthew 9 that struck me recently. 'When he

[Jesus] saw the crowds, he had compassion on them, because they were harassed and helpless, like sheep without a shepherd. Then he said to his disciples, "The harvest is plentiful but the workers are few. Ask the Lord of the harvest, therefore, to send out workers into his harvest field"' (Mt. 9:36–38). Now, why did Jesus ask his disciples to pray this? Surely he could do that? He was the one feeling the compassion, and wouldn't one prayer of his be more effective than all of theirs? But he wants them to *join in with him*, to be co-workers and participants in the divine, compassionate, outgoing, missional life he shares with his Father in the Spirit.

12

The Spirit Brings us Together in Fellowship With God

There is one more point to make about the Spirit: he is the Spirit of fellowship. He stirs up the love the Father and the Son have for each other, and he brings together a family for the Father. As there is fellowship in heaven, so there is on earth. Now at every point we've seen that prayer is simply embracing Christian reality: that we are needy, that we are children of God and so on. But because of the nature of our God, the Spirit doesn't just bring us in Christ to the Father – he brings us *together* to him as the Father's *family*.

Therefore we also pray together with Christ as brothers and sisters before our Father.

Communal prayer, then, is the Christian life in a nutshell – the family of the Father coming together to him to share his concerns. This is why in some ways the prayer meeting is such a battle of flesh against Spirit: will you bludgeon your brothers and sisters with your impressive prayers and actually ignore God, or will you truly go to your Father and seek blessing for them? It can be a formality, a chance to compete with each other – or it can wonderfully foster unity.

> **'Communal prayer, then, is the Christian life in a nutshell – the family of the Father coming together to him to share his concerns.'**

This applies both to praying *for* someone and praying *with* someone. If you pray *for* someone who winds you up, you will find that it's much harder to cherish anger, resentment, suspicion or hatred when you pray for them. Praying *with* someone can also be a powerful experience.

When friends decide to pray sincerely together, perhaps spontaneously, through it you often get to sense an extraordinary, familial closeness with each other. You are being family together. Prayer *for* each other is sharing our Father's compassion. Prayer *with* each other is being family, and it fosters the unity our God loves.

13

Enjoying the Life of God

I hope these truths can encourage you. Prayer is not an abstract activity; it is the chief exercise of faith. It is exercising belief that the Almighty is my willing and kind Father, and that, accepting me in the Son, he wants to hear me and bless me. It is understanding that in fact *each* person of the Trinity is *for* us in our weakness. Our great high priest is filled with brotherly affection for us. Having been tempted himself, he doesn't despise us for being tempted but has compassion and wants to help.

'Our great high priest is filled with brotherly affection for us'

The Son gives us the right to come boldly in his name as accepted children. Then our Father and the Son give us their Spirit precisely to help us enjoy what it is to be children, that is to enjoy the loving, outgoing life of this God.

So Exercise Faith and Pray!

It would be wonderful if you could now find whatever privacy you can to spend time with our Father thinking about your communion with God. Think about what your prayers are actually like. Perhaps it's time for a little self-diagnosis: if prayer is the chief exercise of faith, *why* don't you pray? Be honest. The reasons could be revealing. Do you feel you don't have the time? That's revealing of self-dependence, probably. Do you not see the Father as one you actually want to spend time with? That's revealing, and you'll need a new sight of the glory of Christ to re-awaken faith. Might it be that, deep down, you struggle to believe this truly is the Lord's world? Prayerlessness often indicates that mindset.

Have a think. But as you reflect, be encouraged by one of the psalms:

> *The Lord upholds all who fall and lifts up all* who are bowed down. *The eyes of all look to you, and you give them their food at the proper time. You open your hand and satisfy the desires of every living thing. The Lord is righteous* in all his ways *and* faithful *in* all *he does.* The Lord is near to all who call on him, to all who call on him in truth *(Ps. 145:14–18, my emphasis)*

With this in mind, let's go exercise our faith and pray!

Union

We fuel reformation in churches and lives.

Union Publishing invests in the next generation of leaders with theology that gives them a taste for a deeper knowledge of God. From books to our free online content, we are committed to producing excellent resources that will refresh, transform, and grow believers and their churches.

We want people everywhere to know, love, and enjoy God, glorifying him in everything they do. For this reason, we've collected hundreds of free articles, podcasts, book chapters, and video content for our free online collection. We also produce a fresh stream of written, audio, and video resources to help you to be more fully alive in the truth, goodness, and beauty of Jesus.

If you are hungry for reformational resources that will help you delight in God and grow in Christ, we'd love for you to visit us at unionpublishing.org.

unionpublishing.org

10 Publishing